KINGFISHER EXPLORER BOOKS

UFOs

Jonathan Rutland

Designed by David Nash

Illustrators
Roger Full · Ron Jobson
Angus McKie · Roger Payne · Brian Pearce

KINGFISHER BOOKS

People have reported seeing unidentified flying objects of all sorts of shapes, sizes and colours. The commonest sightings are of glowing balls of light. There are also reports of cigar-shaped objects, egg shapes and 'flying saucers'. This is the best known name given to unidentified flying objects. The large shape on the left is a flying saucer. In 1967 an American barber claimed to have photographed one like it which had been hovering over his house.

The UFO Story

The letters UFO stand for Unidentified Flying Object. UFOs are mysterious flying things. If we knew what they were, they would be IFOs – Identified Flying Objects. An aeroplane is an IFO. So are satellites, kites, balloons and meteors, all commonly mistaken for UFOs.

Many people think that every UFO sighting *must* have an ordinary explanation, even though it is not always possible to find one. Others believe that UFOs do exist and cannot readily be explained away. The popular idea is that UFOs, if they exist, come from space.

Through the centuries, people have observed unusual objects in the sky. From about 1950 these stories were given much publicity in newspapers. The number of reports grew and grew. Many were hoaxes. Many turned out to be distant stars or planets. But there were always a few unsolved mysteries.

Throughout the world organizations sprang up to investigate UFOs. But despite their research we are still unsure whether to be excited or afraid, or whether we should just laugh about UFOs.

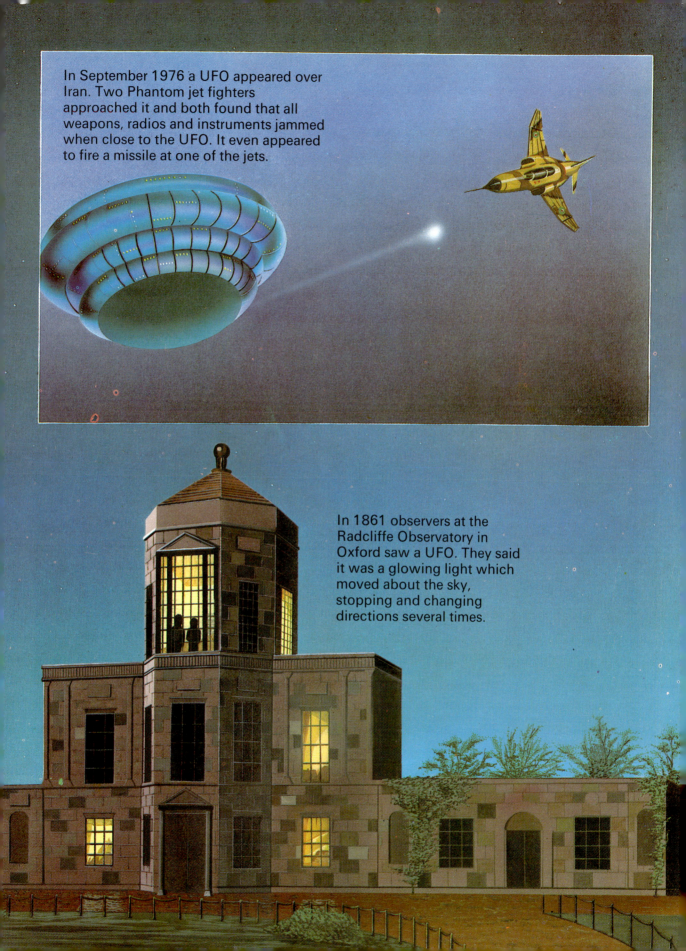

In September 1976 a UFO appeared over Iran. Two Phantom jet fighters approached it and both found that all weapons, radios and instruments jammed when close to the UFO. It even appeared to fire a missile at one of the jets.

In 1861 observers at the Radcliffe Observatory in Oxford saw a UFO. They said it was a glowing light which moved about the sky, stopping and changing directions several times.

The Socorro Saucer

This is one of the most famous stories involving an encounter with a UFO. It happened in New Mexico, USA, on the afternoon of 24 April 1964. A police officer called Lonnie Zamora was chasing a speeding car in Socorro county when he heard a roar and saw a blue flame in the sky. The flaming ball was slowly coming down not far away.

Zamora drew off the road and went to investigate. He spotted an oval silvery-white object. Standing nearby were two human-looking beings. They were about the size of ten-year-old children.

He drove closer to the object, and radioed to his headquarters. Then he stopped and got out of the car. By this time the 'humanoid' creatures had re-entered the craft. There was a slam which sounded like a hatch closing, followed by an ear-splitting roar.

Zamora was terrified and ran back towards the car. He tripped and fell and on glancing back he saw the UFO taking off to the south-west. It sped silently away. Later, investigators found strange burn marks on the ground where the craft had stood.

Illusions and Frauds

Ufologists are people who study UFOs. When they receive a UFO sighting report their first task is to check it carefully to see if the object can be identified. Often there is a simple explanation. All the objects pictured here could be mistaken for UFOs. The strange clouds above look very like flying saucers. They are called lenticular clouds because of their lens shape.

Aeroplanes are sometimes mistaken for UFOs, particularly when the landing lights flash. The ufologist must check what aircraft were in the sky at the time of the UFO report.

UFOs are most often seen at night. Again, the ufologist must

These odd lights are caused by a strange and rare kind of lightning called ball lightning.

The car is out of sight, but its headlights shine on low clouds. The oval shapes look like UFOs.

People thought these were UFOs, but they were geese flying over a city at night, lit up by street lights.

A copy of a fake photograph. The photographer claimed the object was a space ship from Venus.

rule out aircraft, satellites and planets before deciding an object might be a genuine UFO. The brightest planet, Venus, is very frequently mistaken for a UFO.

Man-made UFOs sometimes cause terrific excitement. Security forces throughout southern England were alerted in 1967 when a series of saucer-shaped metal objects were found. They were making weird bleeping noises. But it was all the work of skilled hoaxers and the sound effects were provided by tape recorders.

It is possible to fake UFO photographs, but experts can usually detect hoaxes. Sometimes such photographs show something impossible, like shadows in the wrong place.

Close Encounters

UFO sightings at close quarters are now referred to as close encounters. The term was coined by an American scientist, Dr Hynek, who was adviser to the official American UFO investigation. At first a non-believer, he found that the genuine mystery behind some UFO reports was convincing.

A close encounter of the first kind is a sighting of a UFO which is fairly close. There is no contact with the UFO and it does not land.

In a close encounter of the second kind there are physical

These are pictures of photographs showing UFOs in close encounters of the first kind. Clear photographs are very rare, partly because most UFOs are seen at night.

A close encounter of the second kind. A UFO left a circular mark on the ground. Later snow fell. Then the snow melted, but it did not thaw on the UFO's mark until much later.

traces of the UFO as well as a sighting. For example, people have reported UFOs causing their car engines and lights to fail. If the UFO lands it may scorch the ground or leave prints made by its weight.

The most exciting and extraordinary UFO sighting is a close encounter of the third kind, for living creatures are seen in or near the UFO. Some of them seem to be grotesque little goblins. However most reports say the creatures are like humans, that they are intelligent, but with peculiar skin and clothing.

A close encounter of the third kind. Many witnesses have described the 'ufonauts' (UFO occupants) they say they have seen. These are often like small human beings but with large heads.

Top Secret

Many people think that one possible explanation for UFOs is that they are secret weapons made by the Americans or the Russians. This is most unlikely as such weapons would hardly be tested where they might be seen. And no one has yet built a craft that can suddenly change direction when travelling at very high speed. This is something UFOs seem to do often.

Some UFO enthusiasts think that our governments believe UFOs are from space, but that they do not want us to know. They think we might panic. It is a strange idea, for if we knew UFOs were from outer space, would we really be frightened and expect ufonauts to harm us? It is just as likely that people would be amazed and curious to hear about their world.

In 1938 there was a play on the radio called *War of the Worlds*. It was by the writer H G Wells, and was broadcast in America. The play was about people from Mars making war on our world. Many listeners thought they were listening to the news. What happened is shown below. People ran out into the streets in panic. They were terrified, and rushed off to escape from the Martians who, they thought, intended to kill them. Perhaps the same panic would occur today, if a UFO landed in a major city.

An experimental plane known as the 'flying pancake' was tried out by the US Navy in the 1940s. Seen from below it would resemble a UFO.

Project Blue Book

In the 1950s, people in America were excited and worried about UFOs. There were wild theories that they carried invaders from space, or from Russia. The air force investigation of UFOs was stepped up and renamed Project Blue Book. Thousands of UFO sightings were investigated by the Project officers. About a quarter of the UFOs were satellites or meteors. Another quarter were stars or planets and many were aeroplanes or balloons. But there always remained some mysteries. Blue Book could not explain UFOs away.

The UFO Search

All kinds of different people are interested in UFOs, and the methods of searching for them vary widely.

Many keen amateur ufologists go out into the country to watch for UFOs. They are usually equipped with binoculars and cameras so that if they are lucky enough to see a UFO, they will try to photograph it, record its position, its movements, its size, colour and shape and any other details. They are usually unlucky. UFOs do not seem to appear when one is looking for them.

Some places are particularly favoured by UFO searchers because they have been the scenes of a number of UFO sightings. In Britain, Warminster is UFO country, and in America most sightings have been in the south-eastern states.

Perhaps one day a group of UFO searchers will be lucky enough to have a close encounter like the one pictured on the far right. If they are able to photograph the craft and any occupants, it would provide proof that UFOs are real. At the moment we cannot be certain.

Because we do not know for certain what UFOs are it is difficult to know how to obtain scientific facts about them. But there is an increasing number of scientists who are interested in UFOs. Their access to sensitive listening and recording devices may help provide new knowledge about these phenomena.

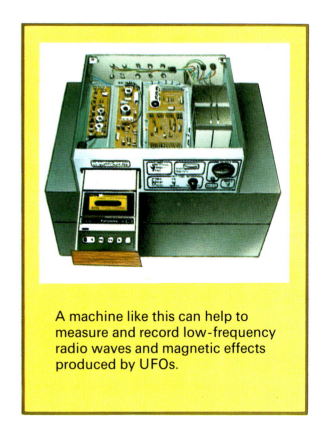

A machine like this can help to measure and record low-frequency radio waves and magnetic effects produced by UFOs.

This ufologist waits by instruments which record sounds, light and radio waves which could indicate the presence of UFOs.

Earthly Flying Objects

Scientists have sent many strange-looking satellites into space, some of which are visible from the ground on a clear night. A large space satellite looks like a bright pin-point of light silently gliding across the sky. It is easy to understand how spacecraft have been mistaken for UFOs.

One day, manned spacecraft may be sent to the other planets in the solar system. They will probably first go to Mars, which is very cold but has a thin atmosphere. The Viking spacecraft which landed in 1976 found no signs of life on Mars, so the crew might take some small living organisms with them, to see if they can survive and spread.

In the future spacecraft might release small living organisms into the clouds of Titan to see if they could survive in such a cold atmosphere.

Another world which spaceships may visit one day is Titan, the largest moon of the ringed planet Saturn. It is far away from the Sun, and colder than the most bitter Siberian winter, but it has a much thicker atmosphere than Mars. Some scientists think that microscopic living things, used to the cold, could live there. They could try to breed cold-resistant organisms in a laboratory, and 'seed' the clouds of Titan with them by launching canisters that break open when they descend.

But before doing this, spacecraft would inspect Titan very closely to make sure that living things really did not exist. They would not want to upset a living world. After all, if visitors from another world dropped new germs into our atmosphere, they could spread over the Earth and cause a terrible plague.

Suppose that some form of intelligent beings exist on a world being examined closely by spacecraft from Earth. Imagine that their world is not very advanced. They do not have radio or television. Nor do they have aircraft or spaceships. To them the spacecraft from Earth would be a complete mystery. They would be 'unidentified flying objects'. Perhaps our puzzlement and sense of mystery about UFOs reported on Earth means that they come from a more advanced world than ours.

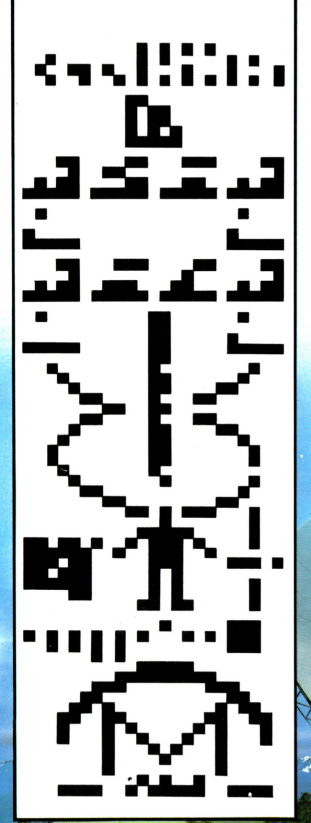

UFOs sometimes show up on radar screens. The arrow points to a 'blip' typical of a UFO as seen on a radar screen.

Right: A time-lapse photograph showing the corkscrew path taken by a glowing UFO in the night sky.

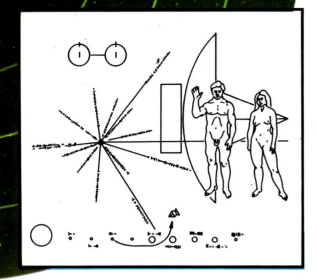

This plaque was attached to *Pioneer 10*, the first spacecraft to leave the solar system. The plaque indicates the craft's origins in case it is found by other beings.

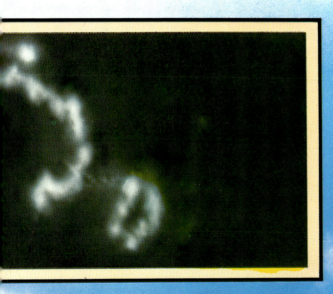

Huge radio telescopes like the one on the left can detect weak radio signals from outer space. They can also send out powerful signals towards far distant stars.

Radio Messages

Are there living creatures anywhere else in the universe? The question is of great concern to ufologists.

There are countless millions of stars in the universe. Many must have planets orbiting them. Many astronomers think there must be life on some of them. The astronomers listen for radio messages from distant planets which might provide proof of life in space.

The problem is much worse than looking for a needle in a haystack. There are so many very distant stars and planets. Also the 'people' of other worlds might be very different from us and they certainly would not speak our language. So what kind of messages might reach us from space and what signals should we send?

One answer is to use the 'language' of computers. The computer message on the far left was sent out in 1974 to a group of stars in the constellation Hercules. It includes a 'picture' of a human being and information on our solar system. However, the message will take 24,000 years to reach its destination so we should not look for a quick answer!

Spaceships

Astronauts have travelled from Earth to the Moon, and robot spacecraft have landed on Mars. But our present-day spacecraft are too slow to take astronauts to the more distant planets in the solar system. To reach the planets of other stars, where ufonauts might live, would take thousands of life-times.

One of the major problems of space travel is the enormous amount of energy needed to escape the Earth's gravity. Huge rockets are needed to launch even the smallest spacecraft. The solution is to build spacecraft in space where there is virtually no gravity. Space stations such as *Skylab* (shown on the right) were built to see if astronauts could live in 'weightless' conditions for long periods.

In the future, manned space stations may circle high above the Earth. Small re-usable 'ferries' like the Space Shuttle will carry crew and materials into space and back. Spacecraft could then be assembled and launched from them. But even at the highest likely speeds, it would take centuries to reach the nearest star.

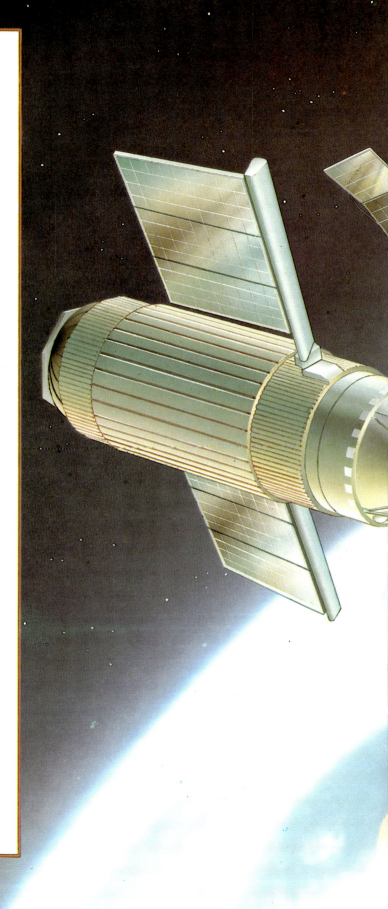

Voyager 2 has sent back information about the giant planets Jupiter, Saturn, and Uranus.

Puzzles and Problems

Can UFOs really be spacecraft from other worlds? If so, where do they come from, and how do they get here?

Our closest neighbours in space are the other planets of our solar system. Astronomers do not think there is life on any of them. This means that UFOs would have to come from the planets of another star. It would take thousands of years for our present spacecraft to reach the nearest star. And most stars are much further away. Even if the ufonauts have spacecraft enormously faster than ours, the journey still seems impossibly long. Unless they have solved the secret of travelling faster than the speed of light – which Earthly science holds to be impossible.

Many ufologists, whilst believing that UFOs exist, do not think that they are interplanetary spacecraft at all. Some, for example, think that UFOs may be time travel machines and perhaps not material in the sense we understand it.

This theory would explain why no UFO has ever been captured. It would also explain why there are so many reports of UFOs which suddenly vanish into thin air.

If ufonauts come from other planets, why are they visiting Earth? If they would land and let us make contact with them all our questions could perhaps be answered.

It is also possible that UFOs come from other universes completely unknown to us. The illustration shows how a ghostly UFO might materialize on Earth from another universe. It would be a dramatic solution to the puzzles and problems of UFOs.

Index

Numbers in *italics* refer to illustrations.

Aeroplanes 4, 5, 8, 9, 13, *13*
Aliens *see* Ufonauts
Astronauts 20
Astronomers 19, 22
Atmospheres 17

Ball lightning *8*
Balloons 4, 13
Britain 5, 9, 14

Cars 8, 11
Close encounters 10–11
Clouds 8
Computers 19

Earth 17, 20, 21, 22

'Flying pancake' *13*
Flying saucers *2*, 3, 6, *7*, 8–9
Frauds 4, 9

Gravity 20

Hercules constellation 19
Hoaxes 4, 9
Humanoids 6, 11, *11*
Hynek, Dr 10

IFO, definition 4
Investigations 4, 6, 8–9, 10, 13, 14
Iran 5

Jupiter 21

Kites 4

Landings 6, *10*, 11
Lenticular clouds 8
Lightning *8*
Light, speed of 20, 22

Mars 12, 17, 20
Meteors 4, 13
Moon 20

New Mexico 6

Oxford 5

Phantom jets 5
Photographs 3, *10–11*, 14, *18*, *19*; fake 9, *9*
Pioneer 10 19
Planets 4, 9, 13, 17, 19, 20–1, 22
Plants 17
Project Blue Book 13

Radar screens *18*
Radcliffe Observatory 5
Radio signals *14*, 19
Radio telescopes *18*, 19
Robot spacecraft 20
Rockets 20
Russia 12, 13

Satellites 4, 9, 13, 17

Saturn 17, 21
Skylab space station 20, *20–1*
Socorro flying saucer 6, *7*
Solar system 17, 19, 20, 22
Spacecraft 17, 19, 20, *21*, 22
Space Shuttle 20
Space stations 20, *20–1*
Stars 4, 13, 19, 20, 22
Sun 17

Telescopes, radio *18*, 19
Time travel 22
Titan *16*, 17

UFO, definition 4
Ufologists 8, 14, 19, 22
Ufonauts 6, 11, *11*, 12, 20, 22
Universes, other 22
USA 3, 6, 10, 12–13, 14
Uranus 21

Venus 9
Viking spacecraft 17
Voyager 2 *21*

Warminster 14
War of the Worlds 12
Weapons, secret 12
Wells, H G 12

Zamora, Lonnie 6

This revised expanded edition published in 1987 by
Kingfisher Books Limited, Elsley House,
24-30 Great Titchfield Street, London W1P 7AD
A Grisewood & Dempsey Company
Originally published in small format paperback
by Pan Books Ltd in 1979.

© Grisewood & Dempsey Ltd 1979, 1987

All rights reserved. No part of this publication
may be reproduced, stored in a retrieval system
or transmitted by any means, electronic,
mechanical, photocopying or otherwise, without the
prior permission of the publisher.

Cover designed by The Pinpoint Design Company

BRITISH LIBRARY CATALOGUING IN PUBLICATION DATA
Rutland, Jonathan
 UFOs. – rev. ed – (Kingfisher
 explorer books)
 1. Unidentified flying objects – Juvenile
 literature
 I. Title II. Rutland, Jonathan. Exploring
UFOs
001.9'42'09 TL789

ISBN 0-86272-302-7

Phototypeset by Southern Positives and Negatives
(SPAN), Lingfield, Surrey
Printed by Graficas Reunidas SA, Madrid, Spain